Marcus Rosenblum

The Story of

Franklin D. Roosevelt

by

MARCUS ROSENBLUM

*Illustrated with photographs,
and with original drawings
by*
FRANCES M. BALL

SIMON AND SCHUSTER NEW YORK

Acknowledgment

The author and the publishers express their appreciation to The Franklin D. Roosevelt Library, Hyde Park, New York, for kind assistance in the collection of photographs for this book and for permission to use certain photographs owned by the Library.

The photograph on the cover of this book is reproduced by courtesy of The Franklin D. Roosevelt Library.

PUBLISHED BY SIMON AND SCHUSTER, INC., ROCKEFELLER CENTER, NEW YORK 20, N.Y.

Contents

‹‹‹‹‹‹‹‹‹‹‹‹‹‹›››››››››››››

Courtesy The Franklin D. Roosevelt Library, Hyde Park, N. Y.

President Roosevelt gives a "fireside chat" (1934)

A Busy Boyhood

CHAPTER 1

SMALL BOY sat writing at a low nursery table. His governess sat beside him, watching. This was important. The little boy was writing a letter to his mother, who was away on a visit.

"My dear Mama," he wrote. "I am in a great hurry. I found two birds nests. I took one egg we are all well. I am going to the Millie Rogers Party and to meet Papa. Goodbye your loving Franklin P.S. love to all."

The little boy was Franklin Delano Roosevelt. He had written his first letter to his mother at five years. That may seem rather young to have learned to write a letter. But Franklin Roosevelt did not wait to enter first grade at six, as most children do. He did not go to kindergarten, or to nursery school. His school came to him at home. He had private lessons from tutors and governesses.

Home to Franklin Roosevelt was a big rambling house set high in the hills that rise above the Hudson River. Vines grew over the pillars of the long porch. Birds nested in the vines and in the bushes and the great trees that shaded the lawns. There was plenty of room for games and fun at Springwood, as the Roosevelt home was called then. But Franklin did not have very much time to play.

Everyone at Springwood was making plans for Franklin. His mother, who was young and beautiful, loved him very much. She hoped Franklin would some day be a great man.

His father did not have to go to work every day as many fathers do. He had time to help plan Franklin's studies, too. And every moment of every day was planned.

There was a time to dress in the morning. There was a time for breakfast, a time for morning lessons, a time for lunch. There were hours set for piano lessons, for French and German lessons. There was a time for riding lessons and drawing lessons and even for learning to shoot. And of course there was always bedtime.

Franklin takes a ride on "Budgy"

Sometimes Franklin felt as if he had too much attention. One day when he was only five years old, he said with a deep sigh, "Oh, for freedom!"

Suddenly his parents realized how hard their little boy worked. "You shall have your freedom, Franklin," they told him. "You may have a whole day to do as you please."

Next morning Franklin kissed his mother goodbye after breakfast and set out for his wonderful day. There were wild flowers in the woodlots. There were birds'

3

nests in the branches above. There were far-off cor-
ners to explore. Franklin came home that evening more
tired and hungry, and certainly dirtier, than he had
ever been.

After that he was satisfied to go back to his schedule.
But he did like to get away once in a while. He always
liked that, all his life. He loved to laugh and to have
fun and to play jokes.

His parents often took their small son traveling with
them. Once when he was five years old, they called
on an old friend of Franklin's father, Mr. Grover Cleveland, who was then President of the United States. This
was Franklin's first view of the White House. Mr.
Cleveland placed his hand on the boy's curls and said,
"My boy, I have a strange wish for you. I hope you will
never be President of the United States."

At home, Franklin spent little time thinking of the
White House. In his free hours he hiked and swam. He
collected naval books, birds, and stamps.

"Please tell Uncle Will that if he has any stamps I
should like to have them as I have begun to make a
collection," he wrote to one of his aunts, when he was
nine.

He rode his own pony, Debby, and he learned to
shoot a gun. He liked to build things, too, in the work-
shop with grown-up tools.

Franklin with his mother in 1887

"I should like to be a farmer," he told his mother one day. "I should like to raise chickens." So he had a small farm and a small chicken house of his own.

5

There were other children in the neighborhood, too. There were birthday parties with games and prizes. And they visited each other's homes to play. Franklin usually planned the games and told the other children what to do. His parents noticed this.

"You must learn to take turns," his mother told him. "The other children have games they would like to play, too. No one likes to have one child always order the rest about."

"But, Mother," Franklin explained, "if I don't give the orders, nothing gets done."

At Hyde Park, Franklin rides "Debby," his first pony

As Franklin grew a little older, he was allowed to read by himself in his father's big library. There he curled up with big books of history and geography, lives of great men, and stories of the sea.

And on long walks with his father he learned about the land surrounding his home. He learned about the rocks that made up the hills above the Hudson. He learned to know the grains and the grasses that ripened in the fields along their walks. And he soon knew the birds and the trees, and the wild flowers that came up in the spring. His love for his home was strong in him all through his life.

Sometimes his walks with his father were far from the Hudson Valley. The Roosevelts went often to Europe. When Franklin was seven, he heard his parents planning their next trip.

"Franklin will go to England with us this year," his father said, and his mother agreed.

Franklin was delighted. For already he loved the tang of salt air and any kind of boat at all.

It was a wonderful voyage. The big ship was a whole exciting new world to explore. And in England there were new friends and playmates waiting. Part of the visit Franklin spent in bed, ill with typhoid fever. But as soon as he could be up and around again, he went to stay at a big country house. There were lively games of soldiers and steeplechase, and dusty chests of old playthings to explore.

Two years later, Franklin visited Germany with his parents. There they lived in a big hotel on a lovely lake at Bad Nauheim. Franklin went to a public school for the first time—to a German school, of course. He studied "German reading, German dictation, the history of Siegfried, and arithmetic in which I am to do 14 x 71 on paper," he reported.

Still he had plenty of time left for shooting in the park with bow and arrow, for drawing for an aunt a book of pictures of the places he visited, and for a gift his father brought him one day—a beautiful big toy sailboat. This was the high point of Franklin's trip, and he sailed it every day on the blue lake.

Away at School

CHAPTER 2

ONCE WHEN Franklin's parents were off on a visit, his governess made him stay in bed because he had a slight fever. He wrote his parents a lively report.

"I am dying of school fever," he said, "and you will be horrified to hear that my temperature is 150°"

A few years later, he had real school fever. For at fourteen, Franklin entered Groton, over the hills in Massachusetts. His mother took him to school and left him there. It was a hard separation for them both, for they had been together so much.

9

Now for the first time Franklin was not the center of his world. Here the rules were stricter than any he had known at home. The upperclassmen treated newcomers almost as slaves, and it was hard for Franklin to accustom himself to this.

He was a serious boy. At first some of the others called him "Uncle Frank." But he learned to love the school and made real friends there.

Soon football games between the near-by prep schools and Groton were the most important events in his life. There were other new interests, too. Photography was one. Franklin took rolls of pictures which seemed to him splendid indeed. He bought an album and mounted the pictures, as everyone did in those days. But he also had a share in a dark room for developing pictures.

He had a handsome green canoe on the river at school, and a toboggan for winter sports.

He took up debating, and loved to take the side of the underdog in questions of the day. He managed Groton teams, and looked very dapper in a straw sailor hat banded in Groton's colors.

But Franklin and his friends did not think that Groton was the whole world. The papers were full of stories of the destruction of the battleship *Maine* in the harbor at Havana, which was then under the rule of Spain.

Franklin (extreme right) *in a play at Groton School (1900)*

There were stories of the dashing Rough Riders who were gathering under Theodore Roosevelt to free the colonies of Spain. It was all the talk among schoolboys at Groton as elsewhere.

Franklin Roosevelt could see himself in a dashing uniform with a hat with a big curling brim. In his mind's eye he was charging up a hill on a fine black horse, waving a sword and shouting encouragement to the fighting men who followed.

"I will join the Rough Riders, too!" he decided. He knew his parents would not be pleased, but he went ahead with his plans in secret. At last came the day to leave.

And Franklin came down with measles.

That was the end of his Rough Riders dream. He stayed on at Groton and was graduated with his parents proudly looking on.

The next fall he went on to Harvard University, where he made the highest score among a thousand who took the entrance examinations that year. He was not a lonely newcomer at Harvard, for his prep-school friends made a tight little group of their own.

Soon he was branching out into school activities. He rowed on the freshman crew. He belonged to six social clubs. He worked on the *Crimson,* the college daily paper. He became so interested in the newspaper that he stayed on an extra year—he had earned his degree in three years—to edit the paper and take advanced courses in government. The editorials he wrote led the school to put in fire escapes and firefighting equipment and to take other measures to protect student health and safety. And the warm interest in newspaper work which he always kept was a help in later years, when he had to deal with so many men and women of the press.

Young Man With a Career

CHAPTER 3

"I SHOULD like to go to Annapolis," Franklin told his family, when it was time to plan his future. "You know how I have always felt about the sea and the navy. I should like to make it my life work."

His family knew well how he felt. He had had his own sailboat since he was fourteen. He was a skilled sailor and navigator. He was so keen about the Navy that as a boy he even memorized many parts of Admiral Mahan's "History of Sea Power." But the Roosevelts did not approve of the Navy as a career for their only son.

13

Franklin followed his father's advice and entered Columbia Law School. Soon after, he married Anna Eleanor Roosevelt, a distant cousin. He had known Eleanor since she was a baby. Now she was a tall, shy girl with a sweet smile, soft blue eyes, and lovely wavy hair. At the wedding, dashing Theodore Roosevelt, once leader of the Rough Riders and now President of the United States, gave the bride in marriage.

Together the couple moved into a small home in New York City. Their first child, a baby girl whom they named Anna, was born while her father was still studying law.

After leaving law school, Franklin worked for a New

Courtesy The Franklin D. Roosevelt Library, Hyde Park, N. Y.

At Campobello with Eleanor Roosevelt, Anna, and "Duffy" (1907)

At Hyde Park with Anna, James, and Franklin, Jr. (1917)

York law firm. Later he formed a partnership with some friends in New York. But now the children were coming along, James and Elliott, and later Franklin Junior and John. Their parents wanted them to have all the fun and wonder of childhood in the country. So they spent much of their time at the old family home in Hyde Park.

Theirs was a lively, happy family. They spent wonderful summers at Campobello Island off the wooded coast of Maine. They rattled around the countryside in one of the earliest Ford cars in their neighborhood. They romped and played together, through the big house and over the wide lawns.

Franklin Roosevelt loved to spend time with his

family. He liked the comfortable country life. He liked to sail and to travel. He liked to pore over his collection of stamps, and to follow his several other hobbies. He had a busy law practice. He had enough money to live as he pleased. Many men would have said, "This is enough."

But Franklin Roosevelt did not live for himself alone. He was interested in public affairs.

In 1910 the Democrats of Hyde Park had a meeting. There were not many of them. Most of the people in the countryside were Republicans. But every time the elections came around the Democrats put up candidates anyway.

"Why don't you run for the State Senate?" they asked Franklin Roosevelt. And he decided he would.

The Republicans did not pay much attention to the Democratic candidate. They were so certain of victory that their own candidate did not bother to talk to the people very much during his campaign.

But Franklin Roosevelt did. He borrowed a red automobile, and he drove up and down the dusty country roads, stopping at school houses and town halls, wherever he could speak to a little group. The Republicans thought this was funny. But the voters did not.

The voters remembered the bright red automobile. They remembered the tall, handsome young man with the flashing smile. And they remembered the warmth with which he said, "If I am elected to the State Senate, I shall go as a servant of the people, never as a slave to party bosses."

This sounded good to the voters, and they remembered it when they cast their ballots. To the amazement of both parties, Roosevelt was elected. And the Republicans did not think it was funny any more.

In Albany, Roosevelt kept on taking his work seriously. He spent long hours in meetings and discussions. And he lived up to his election promises.

He fought the bosses of his own party when they tried to do something he felt was wrong. He stood up to them even when the bosses arranged for Roosevelt's law firm to lose clients, when they told other clients not to pay their bills, when they arrested some of Roosevelt's men and offered to set them free if they would vote the bosses' way. But Roosevelt would not give in. He beat the bosses at their own game.

Roosevelt was learning the art of politics. As Mrs. Roosevelt once said, "Politics is the art of getting things done." Roosevelt was learning how to get things done in government.

One time the voters in his district sent him postcards urging him to vote for a bill which he knew was bad.

"I do not want to vote against the wishes of the voters

who elected me," Roosevelt thought. "I must show them why the bill is wrong."

Roosevelt wrote a letter which he sent to the voters, telling why the bill was wrong. Into each letter he slipped a postcard, stamped and addressed to himself. "Please vote NO on the antivivisection bill" was the message on the card.

When these cards began coming back to him in the mail, Roosevelt knew his letter was convincing the voters. Soon, enough had come back so that he was able to vote against the bill with a clear conscience.

At another time, Roosevelt's friends told him, "If we could delay the vote on this bill for a couple of hours, we would have a good chance of bringing in enough men for our side to win."

"I will take care of that," Roosevelt told them. So for two hours he lectured to the Senate on the bird life of the Hudson Valley until enough men came in to pass the bill.

Franklin Roosevelt was busy learning how to get things done in government. And older men were watching him. "He is a comer," they said. "He is heading for bigger things."

In the Navy

CHAPTER 4

I N 1912, Woodrow Wilson was elected President of the United States. He was the first Democratic President for many years. Franklin Roosevelt had worked hard for his election. Roosevelt was now a recognized leader among the young Democrats.

When the new administration was being set up in Washington, D.C., naturally the planners said, "We want Roosevelt here in Washington."

Wilson's Secretary of the Treasury offered him his choice of two prized financial offices. But Roosevelt was not interested.

19

Then the Secretary of the Navy called him. "Would you like to be Assistant Secretary of the Navy?" he asked.

"Would I like it? I'd rather have that place than any other in public life!" said Roosevelt heartily.

The Navy had long been a chief love of his, and this was his chance to work with it and to guide it. It was his biggest job so far. It was a wonderful chance to show what he could do, and in a field he loved!

"First of all," he decided when he took over, "I want to know where we stand." Roosevelt made a complete survey of the Navy. He did not wait for others to tell him how the Navy was doing. He went to see for himself. When he and his men had checked and visited and studied, he published a report.

It was usual for these reports to say that everything was fine. But Roosevelt said the Navy was doing its work badly. He wanted the United States to have a fine, strong, efficient Navy. And he knew the only way to make the Navy strong was to find its weaknesses and correct them.

Now the weaknesses were known. Roosevelt set about correcting them. He worked long and hard. And he did not always stay safely at a desk in Washington. He went to the ships and stations to see how the improvements were coming along.

In 1915, the Navy lost a submarine off Hawaii. Submarines were as strange then as they were dangerous. The idea of being shut in a small space under water was frightening. And after this tragedy it looked as if no one would dare to set foot in another submarine.

"I want to go out on the next submarine leaving its base," Roosevelt told the men in charge. "I want to see what life in a submarine is really like." And he went. For he would not have been willing to send another sailor underseas if he had not gone himself.

Courtesy The Franklin D. Roosevelt Library, Hyde Park, N. Y.

The Assistant Secretary of the Navy in Washington (1917)

When the United States entered the First World War in 1917, Roosevelt was busier than ever. "There is no time to spare," he kept saying. "We must get things done, and we must do them now." In a world of delays and red tape, he rushed production of new ships and equipment at top speed.

Once the Navy asked a contractor, who was working under personal orders from Roosevelt, to tell them what it would cost to build a much-needed hospital. The contractor sent plans and figures. Then he added, "Enclosed please find photographs of the completed building." While the others were still gathering plans and figures, Roosevelt had had the building put up and made ready for use!

At this time, the submarines of the German Navy were blasting and sinking the ships of the Allies. From their protected North Sea bases, the submarines stole out to torpedo supply ships from America, supply ships that carried badly needed food and arms for France and England.

One day, some men brought to Roosevelt plans for a new underseas mine. It would explode when a submarine came close. There was heated discussion of these mines. Many people thought they were not practical. They said we would need too many of them to do their work. But Roosevelt was all for them.

"Of course we would need vast numbers," he agreed. "Let us make them in vast numbers then. And quickly."

These mines were set in a great net across 250 miles of water. Two hundred German submarines were lost trying to slip past them. Roosevelt also backed the building of small, fast subchasers to patrol the seas. After a while, German submarine crews refused to go out on missions—from which they knew they would not return. Thus the Germans were locked in the North Sea. Supplies sped safely from the United States to Europe. And at last the surviving submarine crews started the famous rebellion in Germany that ended the war.

Before the war was over, the Democrats wanted Roosevelt to run for Governor of New York. "Your record in the Navy Department will make it an easy race for you," they told him.

But Roosevelt had a job to finish.

"While the war is on," he said, "my place is with the Navy."

Many times he asked to be sent into combat. His chief refused because he needed Roosevelt where he was. But Roosevelt sailed on long tours of inspection into dangerous waters. By choice he traveled on a destroyer, though it is the most uncomfortable ship afloat. When he inspected the battle lines in Belgium, he insisted on going where the fighting was heaviest.

On an inspection trip in France (1918)

When the war had been won, the time came for making the peace. Franklin Roosevelt attended the great Peace Conference in Paris. He talked with King Albert of Belgium and with French and British leaders. He was President Wilson's traveling companion on their return from the Conference. He realized, as Wilson did, that there could be no lasting peace unless the nations of the world banded together to outlaw war.

Now the national elections of 1920 came along.

24

"This is the time to elect an administration that will work for lasting peace," people said. Most Americans, particularly the Republicans, thought the way to peace for the United States was to stay at home, to have nothing to do with world problems, and certainly to stay out of the League of Nations.

Others, including Roosevelt and his friends, believed that the United States of America could never stay out of world affairs. This country had become a world leader in trade and exports as well as in politics. Keeping many people at work in this country depended on selling the goods they grew and made, and trading with all the rest of the world.

"We need leaders," they said, "who are willing to work with the people of other nations for lasting peace."

The Democratic Party knew that Roosevelt was such a leader. So the Party nominated him for Vice President of the United States, to run for office with the Presidential candidate, James M. Cox.

Roosevelt was only thirty-nine years old then, which is young for a man to be a national leader. Roosevelt worked hard for that election. He made more speeches than any other Vice-Presidential candidate in history. Mrs. Roosevelt traveled with him and often spoke to groups of women.

The country, however, was not ready then to join hands with other nations. Most Americans thought we would be safer if we worked by ourselves. The voters chose leaders who would "keep us out of foreign entanglements."

Cox and Roosevelt were defeated.

Courtesy The Franklin D. Roosevelt Library, Hyde Park, N. Y.

The Vice-Presidential candidate (fourth from right)
during the 1920 campaign

Illness Strikes

CHAPTER 5

OR A FEW MONTHS, Roosevelt took a rest from politics. It was summer. The Roosevelt family were enjoying the fresh salt breezes that ruffle the island waterways along the coast of Maine. They had all been swimming and had had a happy day together.

That night Franklin Roosevelt developed a sore throat and a high fever. When the doctor came, he gave bad news to the family. Franklin Roosevelt had poliomyelitis, also called infantile paralysis, which poisons the nerves and cripples muscles.

This was the worst enemy he had ever had to face. For weeks he lay ill, fighting the dreadful infection.

27

At Campobello with James and Elliott (1920)

When the fever left, he knew the worst. He could not walk. He could not so much as move a toe.

Then the magic in him did its work. Instead of fading away in discouragement, his courage and will grew stronger. "I am going to walk again!" he vowed. And he did. First he managed with crutches. Then he put away the crutches for canes and a friendly, steadying arm. He drove a car and even managed to ride a horse.

Years later, when he was asked how he developed the patience to stand the strain of the Presidency, he laughed and said, "You learn patience when you spend two years learning to move your big toe again."

He learned firmness of purpose, too. This firmness was a help to him later in the Presidency.

One day, while he lay in bed almost helpless, a friend came to see him and told him about Warm Springs, Georgia. "The pools there are fine for exercising weak muscles," the friend told him. "Many people with your trouble have been helped there."

The Roosevelts talked it over and they went to Warm Springs. There Franklin Roosevelt spent as much time as possible swimming in the warm waters. And his active mind began to create a new life in that resort.

As more people came to Warm Springs, Roosevelt helped the small staff to fix up places for them to stay. He organized the Warm Springs Foundation to help those who could not afford to pay. He saw to it that the patients had good physical care. But more important, he cheered them up and made them feel that they could still enjoy life.

The Warm Springs Foundation continued to be one of Roosevelt's deep interests all through life. He returned frequently for restful vacations and had a small white cottage of his own on the grounds.

Even a severe illness and a long, slow recovery could not end Franklin Roosevelt's political career. While he was still at home in bed, Mrs. Roosevelt went about for him, to meetings and to informal gatherings where people were discussing problems of the day. She came home and reported to her husband. And sometimes she brought friends with her to talk things over with Franklin.

All his life, Roosevelt had had the best that life could offer—wealth, health, friends, a lively and affectionate family, work which he enjoyed and at which he was successful, travel, and hobbies to fill his every hour. He had pitied the poor and tried to help them. But when you have everything, it is hard to feel as people do who do not have enough of anything. Now for a time he had lost his health. For the first time he had to get along without something. It gave him new understanding and new sympathy for others.

He listened with deep interest to the talk of those who were fighting for better working and living conditions for working people. They wanted safe factories, sensible working hours, a living wage, and decent homes. Roosevelt made up his mind that when he could go back into active politics he would fight for these things.

That time came in 1928 while he was still recovering at Warm Springs. Alfred E. Smith, who was running for President on the Democratic ticket, asked Roosevelt to join the campaign as the party's choice for Governor of New York. Smith was an old political friend of Roosevelt's. Roosevelt had nominated Smith as the Democratic Presidential candidate at the party convention in 1920, again in 1924, and once more in 1928. In 1928 he had published a book about Smith, called *The Happy Warrior,* which was widely read and discussed during the campaign. Now Smith, in asking Roosevelt to run for New York's governorship, was putting him in line for one of the most important public offices in the Nation.

Roosevelt thought this over carefully. He talked it over with his family.

"You are gaining strength at Warm Springs," his family reminded him. "If you stay on here, with more treatment you may recover fully. Your most important duty now is to yourself."

Courtesy The Franklin D. Roosevelt Library, Hyde Park, N. Y.

"The Little White House" at Warm Springs (1932)

"No," said his friends. "We want you to be well and strong, too. But your most important duty now is to your state and your party."

They persuaded him at last. He agreed to run for Governor, though, as he said, "Every personal consideration is against it."

His family was sad when the news came. They had always had lively times together, and they prized their family life. Daughter Anna was old enough to vote for her father. The four sons—James, Elliott, Franklin Jr., and John—were all past childhood, but they wanted their father to stay at home.

Roosevelt's mother and the others looked so glum that he laughed and said, "Well, if I've got to run for Governor, there's no use in all of us getting sick over it."

Once again he started out on a busy campaign trip. He met with voters wherever he could. Soon his flashing smile and hearty friendliness were known to people all over the state.

It was a bad year for the Democrats. Al Smith lost the election, even the New York State vote. But Roosevelt was elected Governor.

While he was Governor, Roosevelt again showed his gift for getting things done, for making friends, for encouraging people and getting them to work together. In Albany, he faced many of the problems he was to face later in Washington, and he found ways to meet them and get action on them.

He also had a chance to test out a theory he was later to prove in Washington. You know that government in the United States is divided into several parts: the *executive* (the president of the nation and the governors of the states); the *legislative* (the congress of the nation and the legislatures of the states, which are the lawmaking bodies); and the *judiciary* (the courts and judges who decide what the laws mean and how to enforce them).

Roosevelt thought it was the duty of the Governor (the *executive*) to prepare a program for the government which the lawmakers (the *legislative* body) could approve, change, or turn down. The New York legislature did not agree with Roosevelt, and they went to court on this issue. But the highest court in the state (the *judiciary* branch) said Roosevelt was within his rights.

Later, as President, Roosevelt went ahead with large plans for the government, in this same way. Again many people objected. They said he was taking too much power for himself. Sometimes even the United States Supreme Court decided against him. But as he had said as a little boy, "If I don't give orders, nothing gets done."

Roosevelt wanted the people of New York State to

understand the kind of government he was trying to give them. So he told them about it by speaking to them on the radio. The voters gave him their backing. They reelected him Governor in the next election by a far larger vote than before.

And as Governor of New York, Franklin Roosevelt was being prepared for the biggest job of all.

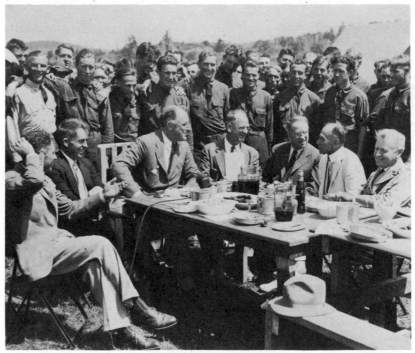

Acme Photo

The new President (at head of table) *at a CCC Camp (1933)*

Depression President

CHAPTER 6

IN 1932, the United States of America, like many other countries of the world, was in what was called the Great Depression. Everything in the business world was at a low ebb. Prices were low, but wages were so low, and so many people were without jobs at all, that people could not buy what they needed. Unsold goods piled up in factories. Because there was no profit in making things no one could buy, many factories stopped work and closed down. Then still more people were without jobs. Still more families had no money coming in to buy food and clothing and pay rent.

Many people who had been rich grew poor. Their savings were lost when stores and factories closed down. Many people who had worked hard all their lives could find no work to do, and their families were hungry. Almost everyone was afraid — afraid of losing money, afraid of losing a job, afraid of not having a place to live or enough to eat.

In the depth of this depression, Franklin Roosevelt was elected President of the United States.

Shortly before he took office in March, 1933, many banks in the country closed down. People were afraid to trust the banks with their money, and banks cannot run when people do not have faith in them. It is hard for business to run without banks. So the business of the country was in a sad state.

In every city, men and women stood in bread lines, waiting their turn at a street kitchen for charity food. In every town and village, people who had always earned their own way were living on "relief" money given them by the county or state. It was a sad, hungry, empty time.

Then into office came Franklin Delano Roosevelt. He promised a "New Deal." He said he would remember "the forgotten man." He said, "We have nothing to fear but fear itself." And he gave the country new hope.

Seldom has a country seen such a busy time as that

first hundred days of the New Deal. Most of the banks opened again. The government guaranteed to stand back of deposits, and people felt it was safe to leave their money in the banks.

The government hired millions of jobless men, women, and boys—it provided useful jobs which built new parks and playgrounds, repaired roads, cleaned forests of dangerous underbrush, brought music and painting into the lives of millions of people.

A plan was set up to keep families from losing their homes through being poor. Measures were taken to keep up prices of farm crops so that the farmers could be sure of enough income to pay for bringing in the crops. A law was passed that men and women might join labor unions without fear of being fired or punished.

Another law was passed to set up an insurance fund for all unemployed, for the aged workers who could not earn a living any more, for widows and orphans who needed money for food, clothes and shelter.

For the first time, the government drew up grand plans for protecting and using the great natural resources of the country—the rivers, the forests, the deserts, the prairies—for the good of all the people.

During that great Hundred Days, everything moved so fast that people could scarcely keep up with all the new organizations in the government. They began to call them by initials. They talked of N.R.A.* and W.P.A., of H.O.L.C.* and A.A.A., of P.W.A. and T. V. A. And Franklin Delano Roosevelt was known across the land simply as F.D.R.

After the Hundred Days, people had time to catch their breath and take a look at the new administration that had been set up. There was fault-finding.

"They had no business to kill those little pigs," many persons said about the Agricultural Administration. Prices for farm goods had gone down so far that experts decided the only way to help the farmers to make a living was to cut down the number of animals and bushels of grain sold, so prices would go up. But many Americans did not approve of destroying food.

"Those fellows on W.P.A. are boondoggling," many persons said, meaning that the projects started to give jobs to people were a waste of time and money. But the men in the government knew it was better for people to work for a living than to have charity handed to them. They put people to work as fast as possible. There were C.C.C. (Civilian Conservation Corps) camps to bring boys out into the open air to do real work in forests, dust bowls, and countryside. There were P.W.A. (Pub-

*N.R.A.—National Recovery Administration; H.O.L.C.—Home Owners Loan Corporation.

lic Works Administration) projects to build badly needed roads, dams, and public buildings.

There were W.P.A. (Works Progress Administration) projects which did all sorts of jobs in the community. They started symphony orchestras and theater groups. They taught women to sew. They built picnic spots. They wrote guide books giving the history and points of interest of different parts of the country.

These projects tried to use the special skills people had. There were so many people to be put to work, and so many projects started so quickly, that of course some were not a great success. But they were all a part of the great battle against hunger and fear.

"That T.V.A. interferes with private industry. It is dangerous to let the government compete with business," said private businessmen, especially in power and light companies. They were speaking of the Tennessee Valley Authority. Its great series of dams was planned to control floods and to provide cheap electric power for an underdeveloped section of the country. Roosevelt and his New Dealers felt that the best future for the country would be the one which gave the richest life to the most people. And electric power is one force which can make life run more pleasantly and profitably.

Roosevelt knew as well as anyone that not all his

plans could work out perfectly. But he felt, as a poet once said, that "low aim, not failure, is the crime."

He called on men who had studied for years the problems he was trying to solve. He decided the country should have a government by experts, men who were not bound to an old political machine or private interests but who had the public welfare at heart.

Of course, these experts did not always do things in the way people were accustomed to in government. Some people made fun of them and called them "Brain Trusters." But these experts were not afraid of big jobs. And they were not afraid to start over and try again, if at first they did not succeed.

"I see one third of a nation ill-housed, ill-clad, ill-nourished," said Roosevelt. And he set to work to do something about it.

Mrs. Roosevelt was a great help and support to the President in his work. She had a warm-hearted and intelligent interest in public problems. She went on many trips around the country to bring back first-hand reports to the President. She was a leader especially in the movement to break down the prejudices which some people have against people of different races and religions. Later, during World War II, the New Deal passed a law to assure all citizens, of whatever race or religion, an equal chance to get and hold a job.

The New Deal did the most in American history to bring water to the desert, so that crops could be grown where none had grown before. Trees were planted on the wind-torn prairies and rutted hillsides to keep the soil from being washed away. Huge dams were built to supply water and electric power where they had been scarce and expensive.

Of course, all these programs cost a great deal of money. "Our grandchildren will still be paying for this," groaned the critics. But Roosevelt felt that money spent to make a sick country well and happy was money well spent.

Courtesy The Franklin D. Roosevelt Library, Hyde Park, N. Y.

The Presidential train stops during a Western trip (1935)

Courtesy The Franklin D. Roosevelt Library, Hyde Park, N. Y.

The President reviews troops in Africa (1943)

War President

CHAPTER 7

ALL THROUGH the 1930's there were rumblings of war almost all over the world. In 1931, Japan invaded Manchuria, and the long struggle between China and Japan began. But we in the United States felt that was no concern of ours. So Japan went ahead developing her war machine

In 1935, Italy invaded Ethiopia. The League of Nations did not approve. It huffed and puffed about punishing Italy, but in the end it did nothing. And we in the United States felt it was no concern of ours. Italy went ahead building her war machine.

In 1936, civil war broke out in Spain. Civil war is supposed to be a struggle between two forces in the same country. Everyone knew that the Germans and Italians were giving planes, tanks, and well-trained troops to support the Spanish fascists. Everyone knew that the Russians were sending arms and that Communists in many countries were recruiting volunteers to help the Spanish Republic. But we in the United States felt it was no concern of ours.

So Germany's war machine rumbled along. In 1938, Germany seized Austria and part of Czechoslovakia.

In 1939, Germany attacked Poland. That was too much for Great Britain and France. They declared war. But still, too many people in the United States thought it was no concern of ours. Europe seemed far away. Europe had always had its wars. Let them fight it out again, without us.

Franklin Roosevelt did not feel that way. He had been re-elected President in 1936. He was straining to lead the country back to prosperity under his New Deal. When there was a slump in the upward climb, his critics blamed it all on him. He had more than a full-sized job at home. But still he worried about affairs abroad.

"We cannot isolate ourselves from the rest of the world," he said. "We are a member of the great family of nations."

Closer and closer came the war. France was overrun and London was ablaze from bombings. German submarines blew up ships off our very shores. Japanese submarines were sighted off California. But still many people in this country thought we were safe behind our oceans, and could keep out of the war.

Roosevelt saw the danger. He and others tried to prepare this country. Congress passed the draft law by a margin of a single vote. Young men by the tens of thousands began to pour into training camps. Khaki uniforms and the navy blue of sailors bobbed up in city streets. New factories sprouted in vacant fields, to build tanks and guns and airplanes and more airplanes.

It was a struggle to convince the Congress that the United States should send weapons to aid friendly nations abroad. But at last the neutrality law was changed, and American supplies began to cross the ocean.

President Roosevelt still talked to the people of the country by radio as he had through all his years in office. His opening words, "My friends," were almost as familiar to most people as the voices of their own families. They could picture the Oval Room of the White House where he sat at his desk, facing the microphone. They could imagine the ship models and sailing prints around him. They could picture to themselves his strong, lined face as he spoke to them. Through these fireside talks, he kept them in touch with what their government was doing.

It was over the radio, too, though not in the President's voice, that the black news of Pearl Harbor reached most of the homes of the nation on December 7, 1941. Excited voices interrupted the music to read the bulletin: "Early this morning, Japanese planes raided our naval base at Pearl Harbor."

The Axis powers—Germany, Italy, and Japan—followed this attack with a formal declaration of war against the United States.

Now Americans worked harder and faster than anyone would have thought possible. They speeded shipping and food and medicine. And they speeded the orders, the plans and the rules that smoothed the way for all the men and ships and supplies.

Lights burned later than ever in the White House. For it was far more than a busy home, ringing with the shouts of lively Roosevelt grandchildren. The President still found time for a few happy hours with his family, but they were rare. He might call in an old friend to browse with him through the bulky albums of his beloved stamp collection, but that was seldom. He still managed to spend some time swimming in his pool, for that was necessary exercise.

Once in a while, he broke away for a few days of fishing or boating with old friends. Out on the water, dressed in old, comfortable clothes, he was at his best, always ready with a smile and a joke. He knew the secret of enjoying himself. He could relax completely and go back to work with fresh energy. But most of his time during the war was given to the hard tasks of the Presidency.

And the tasks were hard indeed, for the President of the United States is also Commander-in-Chief of its Army and Navy. He met with the chiefs of the Army and the Navy about war plans, with officials of the State Department, with the men in charge of producing weapons and supplies for our forces, with ambassadors and ministers from the Allied countries. And he met with reporters from the nation's newspapers. Franklin Roosevelt had always enjoyed talking with newspaper men. And he knew how important it was for the readers of newspapers to learn what was going on in the world.

His work day started at nine in the morning when he read the newspapers over breakfast in bed. Then from ten to five or five-thirty in the afternoon, there were meetings. Lunch was usually served on a tray in his office. Three times a week, he left early for a swim and massage before dinner. After dinner, there were more reports to hear and read and people to see.

That was his workday in Washington. But he did not

always stay at home. Early in the war, he made a coast-to-coast tour, visiting war plants and Army and Navy stations in half the states of the country.

And there were overseas trips to meet with the heads of other governments, our Allies. Roosevelt and the British Prime Minister, Winston Churchill, met a number of times. Their first and most famous meeting took place at sea, on the battleship *Augusta,* in the summer of 1941. There the two leaders made a list of aims for the peace to come. These aims became known as the Atlantic Charter.

Later they met with Chiang Kai-shek, the Generalissimo of China. They met in Egypt, at Cairo, to talk about defeating Japan, and again at Yalta on the Black Sea.

Roosevelt also traveled to Teheran, in Persia, for a meeting with Josef Stalin, Premier of Russia. Roosevelt, Churchill, and Stalin discussed plans to carry the war to victory and to make certain that peace would last.

There had been gloomy days for the Allies in the early part of the war. Japan swept over our Pacific bases. Germany held most of Europe. But gradually, as Britain and Russia stood firm, and as our guns and planes and men and food crossed the seas in a steady flow, the tide turned. And Roosevelt watched the enemy weaken.

But the war put a great strain on the tiring President.

Roosevelt and Churchill discuss the Atlantic Charter (1941)

He had worries not only abroad but at home, too. There were his four sons, all in the armed services. There was the regular, vast business of government to be watched over. And there was the election campaign of 1944.

Back in 1936, after his first term as President, Roosevelt had run for re-election and won a sweeping victory. The people wanted more of the New Deal. Again in

1940, he agreed to run for re-election, because his party wanted him to lead the nation in the dangerous years ahead. He won this campaign for a third term, though it cost a bitter struggle. Many Americans believed that no man should be President more than two terms. George Washington had been against it, and no other President had ever served a third term. Even men and women who had worked with Roosevelt for years and were his friends, felt that giving so much power to one man for more than eight years was dangerous for our democracy.

Now it was 1944—another Presidential election year. Many people believed peace would come within a year or two. Roosevelt, remembering World War I and the peace that failed, believed that this time America should lead the world's nations in making the coming peace. Although tired and worn after three Presidential terms, he decided to run for a fourth term.

Again, after a hotly fought campaign, he was re-elected. The majority of American voters believed that Roosevelt's leadership would be as valuable in peace as it had been in war.

When he took office for his fourth term, Roosevelt faced a discouraging scene. The war had shattered Europe. A great common task of repair called for action. But the President could no longer depend on the support of Congress. Many men and women who had supported the President only because the nation was at war, turned against him at the first sign of peace. Even old "New Dealers" felt it was time for a change in the government. The Republican Party grew stronger. The President found it much harder than in the old days to win approval of the laws he wanted.

Still, Roosevelt saw with joy the tides of war turning back. He came back from Yalta weary but happy in the knowledge that the war would soon end in victory. He knew that our scientists were completing their secret work on the atomic bomb, the most powerful weapon the world had ever known.

Perhaps that is why his eyes and thoughts were turned far ahead.

"World government is our only chance for lasting peace," he said. "We nations must learn to live and work peaceably with each other instead of fighting among ourselves."

It seemed likely that the peak of his life's work might come as the head of such a world government. For he was the four-time President of the most powerful state on earth. He had made friends with the heads of governments of the two other most powerful states. Above all, people all over the world knew and trusted him. He hoped to justify their trust.

But shortly before Germany surrendered, Franklin Roosevelt's tired body gave way. He was at Warm Springs, Georgia, resting from his travels on behalf of world peace. He was posing for a portrait. He had been signing state papers and chuckling with the artist. Suddenly he fainted in his chair. That afternoon he died.

At the news of his death, men and women all over the world bowed their heads in grief. They had lost a friend. As one young soldier said, "I felt that he knew me. And I felt that he liked me."

Roosevelt was strong. He had faith, intelligence, courage, and a great heart. He knew that there would always be many who saw things differently. Sometimes he became impatient. When he was sure he was right, it was not easy to accept what seemed wrong.

He never let discouragement or weariness or hard work dim his dream of the Four Freedoms for the people of the world:

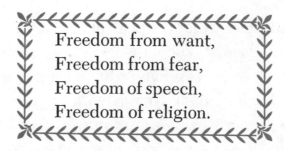

Freedom from want,
Freedom from fear,
Freedom of speech,
Freedom of religion.

And in the hearts of millions, this dream lives on.